EGYPTIAN MYTHOLOGY

SETH

BY HEATHER C. HUDAK

CONTENT CONSULTANT
KASIA SZPAKOWSKA, PhD
PROFESSOR EMERITUS OF EGYPTOLOGY

Kids Core

An Imprint of Abdo Publishing
abdobooks.com

abdobooks.com

Published by Abdo Publishing, a division of ABDO, PO Box 398166, Minneapolis, Minnesota 55439. Copyright © 2023 by Abdo Consulting Group, Inc. International copyrights reserved in all countries. No part of this book may be reproduced in any form without written permission from the publisher. Kids Core™ is a trademark and logo of Abdo Publishing.

Printed in the United States of America, North Mankato, Minnesota.
052022
092022

Cover Photos: Shutterstock Images, background; Olga Chernyak/Shutterstock Images, Seth
Interior Photos: Shutterstock Images, 4–5, 17, 18, 29 (top); Vladimir Zadvinskii/Shutterstock Images, 6, 28 (top); Alex Anton/Shutterstock Images, 8; iStockphoto, 9, 26, 29 (bottom); Chronicle/Alamy, 10; Werner Forman/Universal Images Group/Getty Images, 12–13; Christopher Bellette/Alamy, 14, 28 (bottom); Prisma/UIG/Universal Images Group/Getty Images, 20–21; Peter Hermes Furian/Shutterstock Images, 23; Prisma/PHAS/Universal Images Group/Getty Images, 24

Editor: Layna Darling
Series Designer: Ryan Gale

Library of Congress Control Number: 2021952327

Publisher's Cataloging-in-Publication Data

Names: Hudak, Heather C., author.
Title: Seth / by Heather C. Hudak
Description: Minneapolis, Minnesota: Abdo Publishing, 2023 | Series: Egyptian mythology | Includes online resources and index.
Identifiers: ISBN 9781532198724 (lib. bdg.) | ISBN 9781644947807 (pbk.) | ISBN 9781098272371 (ebook)
Subjects: LCSH: Seth (Egyptian deity)--Juvenile literature. | Egypt--Religion--Juvenile literature. | Gods, Egyptian--Juvenile literature. | Mythology, Egyptian--Juvenile literature.
Classification: DDC 932.01--dc23

CONTENTS

Seth was a warrior, often shown as an animal.

CHAPTER 1

GOD OF THE DESERT

Seth was a fearless warrior. He helped the king of the gods, Ra. The sun was Ra's boat. He would sail it across the sky from dusk to dawn. But Ra was attacked by a serpent at the same time every night. The large snake wanted to stop the sun from rising.

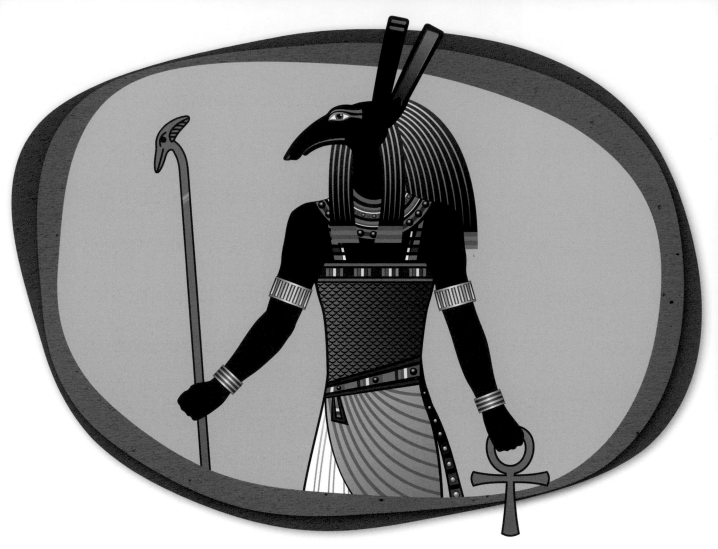

Seth defended the king of the gods, Ra.

Seth defended Ra against the evil monster. He rode on the front of Ra's boat. He used a spear to drive the serpent away. By doing this, Seth made sure the sun would rise. But the serpent came back night after night.

Seth bragged that he was the only god brave enough to fight off the serpent. He told Ra that he needed to be treated with respect. If not, Seth would cause terrible storms. Over time, Ra grew tired of Seth and sent him away. Ra asked other gods and goddesses to help protect him instead.

Demon God

Some ancient Egyptians believed Seth was a demon. Seth was often shown with red hair or as a mythical creature. The color red represented extreme power. Ancient Egyptians associated the color red with Seth. They believed Seth brought chaos to their peaceful society.

Some of ancient Egypt's structures have lasted for thousands of years.

Ancient Egypt

The ancient Egyptian **civilization** formed more than 5,000 years ago in northern Africa. Ancient Egyptians left many clues about how they lived. Their temples, tombs, artwork, **mummies**, and statues tell people today about their ways of life. Ancient Egyptians told epic

Egyptian temples left behind clues about ancient Egyptians' ways of life. Carvings at the Temple of Edfu tell stories about Seth.

stories about life on Earth and what happened to the soul after death. They also told tales to help explain the world around them. These stories are known as Egyptian myths.

Stories about gods like Seth, *left*, explained the world around the ancient Egyptians.

Gods and goddesses were a big part of Egyptian myths. The ancient Egyptians believed there were hundreds of gods. The gods watched over human souls as they made their way from one life to the next. One of the most powerful gods was Seth. He was the god of **chaos** and war. He controlled the deserts and storms. Seth brought disorder to the world. He was both loved and hated by the people of ancient Egypt.

Further Evidence

Look at the website below. Does it give any new evidence to support Chapter One?

Ancient Egypt

abdocorelibrary.com/seth

Seth, *pictured here as an animal*, was one of the most important Egyptian gods.

CHAPTER 2

WORSHIPPED AND FEARED

Seth was one of the first Egyptian gods. He was the son of Geb and Nut. Geb was the god of Earth. Nut was the goddess of the sky. They were both very powerful. They had three other children, Isis, Nephthys, and Osiris.

Pharaohs like Ramesses III, *center*, believed Horus, *left*, and Seth, *right*, could give them power.

Seth was an important god. He was the god of the desert. Most of Egypt was covered by desert. It was a harsh place. Ancient Egyptians thought Seth controlled the wild animals that lived in the desert. He could bring sandstorms and flash floods to the land. Seth was strong and dangerous. People both worshipped and feared him.

Good or Evil?

In early Egyptian myths, Seth was a hero. People prayed to him to help their dead family members get to the afterlife. Seth blessed and protected the dead.

Some pharaohs even took on the name Seth. They believed the god gave them power. Sometimes the pharaohs would call on Seth for help.

Over time, Seth became known as god of darkness and evil. He was jealous of his older brother, Osiris. Osiris ruled over all of Egypt. Seth wanted his brother's throne. He made a beautiful chest and tricked Osiris into getting inside. Seth then sealed the lid and threw the chest in the Nile River.

Harmony

Ancient Egyptians believed everything had an opposite. This was the only way to have balance and harmony. The god Horus was Seth's opposite. Without Seth's chaos, Horus could not bring order. Horus was good and represented light. Seth was evil and represented darkness.

Seth was a symbol of chaos for ancient Egyptians. They believed he could cause disasters like floods.

God of Chaos

Seth's rule brought chaos to Egypt. He became a symbol of all things feared by the ancient Egyptians, such as storms, **droughts**, war, hunger, and invaders from other countries. People did whatever they needed to survive the problems Seth brought to them. Some even turned on one another.

Seth, *left*, was the enemy of Horus, *right*.

Seth was the enemy of many other gods. Finally, Seth's nephew Horus fought him for the throne. It was a battle of good versus evil. In their final fight, Seth turned into a hippo. He attacked Horus's boat. Horus speared Seth. Horus then took over the throne.

Professor Richard Wilkinson wrote this quote about Seth:

> Seth was the "Red One," the ill-tempered god who personified anger, rage and violence, and who was often regarded as evil personified.

Source: Richard H. Wilkinson. *The Complete Gods and Goddesses of Ancient Egypt.* Thames & Hudson, 2003. 197.

Comparing Texts

Think about the quote. Does it support the information in this chapter? Or does it give a different perspective? Explain how in a few sentences.

Many pharaohs, like Ramesses II, *center*, worshipped Seth, *left*.

CHAPTER 3

THE EVIL ONE

The ancient Egyptians admired Seth's power. But they were also afraid of him. Seth could cause pain and suffering. People prayed to Seth so he wouldn't harm them. They asked him to hold off storms and droughts.

Worshipping Seth

Seth was sometimes called Nubti. Nubt was a city in ancient Egypt. It was the main place of worship for Seth. The Temple of Seth was built there in his honor. Ruins of the temple can be seen there today.

Other temples for Seth were built all across Egypt too. His image was carved into the stone walls of some temples. But most were destroyed as Seth became known for evil rather than good. Statues, images, and other reminders of Seth were removed from many places of worship.

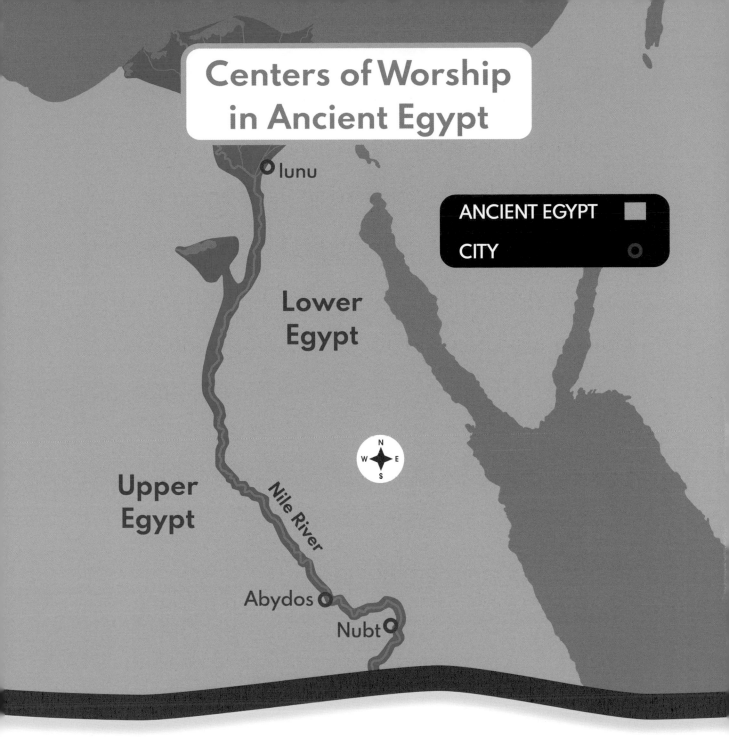

Centers of Worship in Ancient Egypt

O lunu

Lower
Egypt

ANCIENT EGYPT ☐
CITY ◎

Upper
Egypt

Nile River

N
W E
S

Abydos O
Nubt O

Some gods and goddesses had main worship centers. Nubt was the main place of worship for Seth. Iunu, today called Heliopolis, was the main place of worship for Ra, the sun god. Abydos was the main place of worship for Osiris, the god of the dead.

This statue of Seth was most likely sculpted some time between 1300 and 1080 BCE.

Ancient Egyptians held festivals that involved Seth. One took place just before the start of each new year. People celebrated the births of some of the most important gods. Seth was one of them. Another festival honored Horus's victory over Seth. It involved a play. Actors pretended to spear a hippo that was meant to be Seth. People would eat a hippo-shaped cake at the end of the festival.

Mythical Creature

Seth is often shown as a beast with square-tipped ears and a forked tail. He has red hair. Ancient Egyptians thought red was the color of extreme power. No one knows for sure what kind of animal Seth was meant to be. Some people think it was a mythical creature.

Seth is often shown as having a long-snouted animal head and a staff.

Seth Today

Images of Seth are commonly seen in Egypt today. Pictures of him are carved on temples. These images show some of the myths that involve Seth. Stories of Seth were first told thousands of years ago. His role as the god of chaos has made him an important part of Egyptian mythology.

Explore Online

Visit the website below. Does it give any new information about ancient Egypt that wasn't in Chapter Three?

Egyptian Gods

abdocorelibrary.com/seth

LEGENDARY FACTS

Seth defended Ra's sun boat. He would use a spear to drive a serpent away. By doing this, Seth made sure the sun could rise.

Seth was Horus's opposite. Seth brought chaos to Horus's order.

Seth's rule brought chaos to Egypt. He became a symbol of all things feared by the Egyptians, such as storms, droughts, war, and hunger.

In artwork, Seth takes on animal forms. He is often seen as a beast with a long snout.

Glossary

afterlife
in ancient Egypt, a place where a person's spirit goes after death

chaos
disorder and confusion

civilization
a complex, organized society

droughts
periods of little or no rainfall

harmony
balance and agreement

mummies
bodies of humans or animals that have been preserved to prevent decay

pharaohs
rulers of an Egyptian kingdom; kings

Online Resources

To learn more about Seth, visit our free resource websites below.

Visit **abdocorelibrary.com** or scan this QR code for free Common Core resources for teachers and students, including vetted activities, multimedia, and booklinks, for deeper subject comprehension.

Visit **abdobooklinks.com** or scan this QR code for free additional online weblinks for further learning. These links are routinely monitored and updated to provide the most current information available.

Learn More

Drimmer, Stephanie Warren. *Ancient Egypt*. National Geographic, 2018.

Krekelberg, Alyssa. *Horus*. Abdo, 2023.

Index

About the Author

Heather C. Hudak has written hundreds of kids' books on all kinds of topics. She loves to travel when she's not writing. Hudak has visited about 60 countries and hopes to travel to Egypt one day. She also enjoys camping with her husband and many pets.